Disney Junior

Fun with FRIENDS

Look and Find

pi kids

phoenix international publications, inc.

Mickey and his friends are getting ready to go someplace far away! They can't get there in the Toon Car or the Glove Balloon. Can you guess where the Mousekefriends are going? Look for these things the Clubhouse pals will need on their trip:

camera

space boots

star chart

astronaut food

rocket fuel

space helmet

Super cheers! The Mousekenauts are deep in outer space! Can you help them find these shining objects floating around?

Jupiter

Saturn

Earth

Mars

the Milky Way

a comet

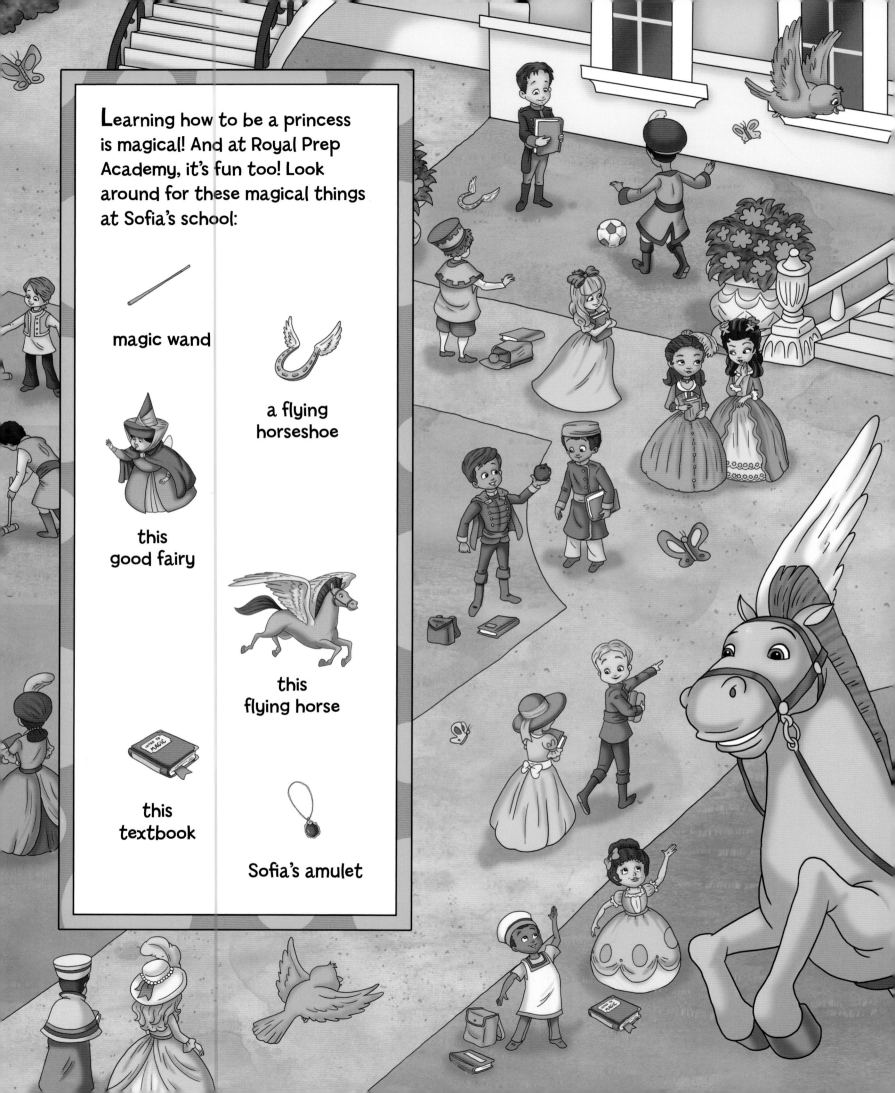

Learning how to be a princess is magical! And at Royal Prep Academy, it's fun too! Look around for these magical things at Sofia's school:

magic wand

a flying horseshoe

this good fairy

this flying horse

this textbook

Sofia's amulet

Sofia is ready for the royal ball and banquet. She has learned dances and manners, and even a few magical spells from Cedric! Help her find these royal things:

the King's crown

Sofia's tiara

crystal goblet

flute

royal portrait

fancy shoes

Doc McStuffins' clinic is busy today! She is giving all her toys a checkup to make sure they're feeling their best. Find these things to help Doc do a good job:

stethoscope

air pump

sponge

doctor's bag

reflex hammer

otoscope

Doc and her best friend Emmie are playing in the park. Look for these things they will need for a fun day together:

this ball

jump rope

water bottle

sunscreen

this
sand bucket

inline skates

Ahoy, mateys! Jake and his crew are looking for treasure. X marks the spot! Can you find these things to help Jake outsmart Captain Hook?

telescope

net

lantern

sword

fishing rod

compass

Yo ho, let's go! It's time to return to Pirate Island. Make sure Jake has all these treasures before *Bucky* sets sail:

scuba mask

boomerang

slingshot

message in a bottle

unicycle

drum

Rocket back to the Clubhouse to find and count these things:

1 telescope

2 globes

3 posters

4 books

5 crescent cookies

6 alien toys

Float back to Mickey and his friends in outer space and find these other space-y things:

space gloves

Space Academy decal

two-way radio

astronaut badge

notebook and pencil

this satellite

Fly back to Royal Prep and find these colorful things:

yellow feather

green fan

orange bow

purple butterfly

blue hat

red apple

Twirl back to Sofia's grand ballroom and find these patterns:

polka dots

stripes

zigzags

checkerboard

flowers

plaid

Go back to Doc's waiting room and see what you can find in these places:

next to Lambie

under a blanket

inside Doc's pocket

on the desk

in front of the desk

above the sofa

Skip back to the park with Doc and find these things that rhyme:

rock / sock

duck / truck

log / frog

pail / snail

hat / bat

bee / tree

Paddle back to the Never Land waterfall and look for these pairs:

pair of fish

pair of boots

pair of birds

pair of seashells

pair of flippers

P is for pirate! Sail back to *Bucky* and find these other things that begin with the letter P:

pineapple

pillow

pail

paddle

pearl

palm tree